DIE HARD
RAIDER FANS

DIE HARD RAIDER FANS

Go! Oakland Raiders!
Raider Cat! (Meow)!

Traci Gaines (Raider Cat)

To order additional copies of this book, contact:
Xlibris Corporation
1-888-795-4274
www.Xlibris.com
Orders@Xlibris.com
33692

Acknowledgements

This book is dedicated to all the Raider Fans out there! I want to thank all my Myspace Raiderfans, Chris D., The Official Gorilla Rilla, AfroDeesiac, Beach Lover, K.J. Boopy, Freakin Rican, Ms. Asian Persuasian, Viktoria, Royal Blue, Inferno, Los Raider, The Guardian, Dago Raider, The official, Mr. Fro, Tchiya, Raider-Fan, Knights of, Raidersoulja in Iraq of the RaiderNation, Oaktown Villan, Duo of Danger, High Class and Prostuff

Table of Topics

These are just some of the topics in the book. I always want you all to just read the book from front to back. I always want you all to have something to talk about. I also want you to get out to the games every once in a while. I am actually a security guard for SMG during the Raiders games. I have worked there for about three years now. I have met lots of football, movie, and singing stars who come to the games. I have had a lot of fun fussing with my 49er(whiner) friends, and meeting many other fans from other teams. You've got to admit without them there would be no football. It's all in fun, and I love to hear the roar of the crowd. I also love meeting people as Raider Cat and I have signed many autographs.

4/3/05

Introduction

This book is about all the fans I know and have come to love! Beneath that hard exterior there are hearts of gold, and I want to tell my story. I spoke to BlackHole Rob and told him of my wanting to write the book, he said great but he liked the mystique and roughness that we all portray. I told him yeah I know, but I want to let people know that there are a lot of good, dedicated people that come to the games every season. he told me, "Good Luck!" I have known him since 2002, and he has gone through a lot trying to own the title to the Black Hole but I told him that it would work out, and it did. I always ask how he is doing and he always looks so proud. I had him to sign my shirt one time at Ricky's, we were there for a gathering of the big wigs and the costume people. He couldn't believe it, that I had asked him to sign the shirt, but he did. He said he felt like a celebrity, I told him, "You are!" All the costume people were there, Afrodesiac, Raider Cat(myself), The Pirates(Big Stars Of The Games), Gorilla Man, Senior Raiderman, Shieldhead, StonerDude(From the Famed Raider Fan Radio, and His Band RaiderHead), Krunch, and a few more people. We were there to make an espn commercial. What a day!

Die Hard Raider Fans

You know I have to say that the Raider fans are the most dedicated people I have ever been around in my life. I have met people who have been dedicated to the Raiders for twenty+ years. We've had two people who have sorry to say pass away, we miss them very much, who wanted to have their ashes buried at the BlackHole now if that Isn't dedication, I don't know what is. I have met lots of fans who didn't even turn away when they went to L.A. Their, of course, are fans from all walks of life. I love that fact that the fans can tolerate having fun at tailgate, and then going into the game. We all know it can be back and forth sometimes with very different emotions. Their ahead, their behind, somebody fumbles, their up in the first quarter and behind in the fourth. No one can predict what's really going to happen. I hope this year they go to the superbowl 2005 and shock the world. I have always wanted Oakland to have all winning teams, Raiders, Warriors(who are on fire right now), and the A's. It is always an interesting year for me, I work security for most of the games. I have done this for three years now, and I started to work for the Coliseum because I loved it my whole life. I started working the first year and found out finally that it was basically for people who needed a second job, or for extra money if they were going to college. It has been a wonderful three years, some people get upset, but it's still worth it.

Well it's now 2006. Sorry to say we have had four deaths, pizza man, rob, raider man, and hardcoreR8R. There was also a woman from the Oakland Raiders Booster Club, that passed away also, a long time fan. Rob and I had grown up together as little kids. It wasn't until I came to the tailgate in 2002 that I saw him again. Afrodesiac was a part of the tailgate with him and Winn. The night Rob died he was in front of his house sitting on his motorcycle when a lime green cadillac hit Rob killing him instantly. With Raiderman, he was at home with his mom watching the game, and a bullet came through the front window of his home, struck him in the forehead and killed him instantly. As far as hardcore, he was in a three car pile up, and tried to move his car out of the way. He was then struck by a vehicle, and killed instantly. These deaths have been pretty hard on me, lately. I was able to take pictures with, or of them myself. I'm known as RaiderCat but I also carry my camera most of the time. I am proud that I was able to meet and be around these wonderful people! There is now another raider fan named skates, sorry to say he passed away in his sleep. There is also another dear friend of mine, Dondada. Sorry to say he did from asthma, they told me. He introduced himself to me as Don. He always had a good time listening to us sing karaoke. He was great at dancing. He was a really sweet guy that sorry to say passed away young, before 40. Craig Allen Long was playing with his daughter. He went outside to get some air and collapsed. He is survived by his wife and daughter.

Ricky's Sports Theater Bar and Grill in the main room 8 raiders jerseys. Stabler, Villapiano, Atkinson, Vella, Plunkett, Bradshaw, Jackson, and Porter. There are 6 tv's with one big screen. In the VIP room there are 6 tv's, and one big screen. There are 6 jerseys Hubbard, Tatum, Martin, Dolby, Sistrunk, and Lominca. 4 hall of fame pictures and they are Ben Davidson 83, Jack Tatum 32, Jim Otto 00, Fred Biletnikoff 25. There are pictures of Skel and Shieldhead. In front there are 3 TV's. The first game is at 9:00, it is the Buffalo Bills and the Chicago Bears. 1st quarter and 7 minutes to go, Chicago 3 and Buffalo 0. On the other TV's, 1st quarter Miami 0 and New England 3, St. Louis 7 and Greenbay 6, Washington 0 and New York 0. 2nd quarter, 13 minuites to go, St. Louis 7 and Greenbay 10. Second quarter 13 to go, Washington 3 and New York 0. 2nd quarter 13 to go, Miami 0 and New England 3. 2nd quarter 14 to go, Chicago 6 and Buffalo 0.

I spoke with Lee "The F lea" Phillips who was the photographer for the Raiders. 2nd quarter 4 minutes to go, Chicago 27 and Buffalo 0, St. Louis 7 and Greenbay 10, Washington 3 and New York 6, Miami 7 and New England 13. While watching, it was Miami 10 and New England 13 at the halftime mark. After halftime, Washington 3 and Newyork 9, Chicago 27 and Buffalo 0, St. Louis 14 and Green Bay 10. It is 3rd quarter, Miami 10 and New England 13, Washington 3 and New York 16, St. Louis 14 and Greenbay13, Chicago 30 and Buffalo 0. 4th quarter, 14 minutes to go, Chicago 30 and Buffalo 0, St. Louis 17 and Greenbay 13, Washington 3 and New York 16, Miami 10 and New England 13. Final score Washington 3 and New York 19, Chicago 40 and Buffalo 7, Miami 10 and New England 20, St. Louis 23 and Greenbay 20. For the Raiders game it is 49ers 7 and Raiders 3 in the first quarter. 2nd quarter Raiders 6 and 49ers 7. 2nd quarter and 21 seconds to go, Raiders 13 and 49ers 7. Then there is the score for halftime, Raiders 13 and 49ers 7. 4th quarter it is Raiders 13 and 49ers 31. 4th quarter and 6 minutes to go, Raiders 20 and 49ers 31. The final score was Raiders 20 and 49ers 34. Boo! I'm a Raider fan.

Ken says, "Why stay at home when you can come to Ricky's, it's like being at the game." We are watching Dallas and Washington. The game is Washington 5 and Dallas 0 in the first quarter with 4 minutes to go. There are 39 men, 5 women including myself, and 4 kids. There are 2 fans rooting for Washington, all the rest like Dallas. It's funny because Washington is playing like the Raiders a little, I'm just being real! Nobody's perfect but friends have said to me that the Raiders need to quit partying. But if you think about it, during a game there are always ups and downs. When the crowd loves the play they get very loud. When a player messes up they call the play, tell the players what to do, and the refs what to do. When the ref says what they like, they all clap and yell, Yeah! It is so cool! After I made that comment there was a fan who said that Washington was acting like the Raiders. One of the kids is occupying his time by playing video games. One guy has lists and his laptop. I guess he's collecting stats. They also root for other teams. They're rooting for Miami because they say that Chicago is an over-rated team. They all stood up and cheered when their team had a great play. When the play is not good they act just like Raiders fans. When Washington gets a touchdown, Dallas fans can hear nothing, but one washington fan yelling, "What's the score now?" They had Randy Moss on the TV, who almost pulled a TO. There are two beers during the game at McAfee(now Orac le). The final scores were Washington 22 and Dallas 19.

I arrived at Nikko's restaurant for 7:30a.m. I met the director and crew for the commercial. There are 2 actors wearing costumes. One ia a hare and the other is the tortoise. There are 3 actors besides myself. We are called extras. There is one guy that says he prefers to be called background actors. There are customers coming back and forth into the restaurant. We're now discussing issues from the voting pamphlet. There is one guy that had to read the paper and drink coffee. We had to stay until 4:00p.m. There are 6 hours left. It turns out that was the Fast Trak commercial. The actors were really great. I met Mr. Fruge(frujay), and he introduced me to my acting coach. I have had only one private lesson so far. I will return to have another one soon. The coach is great, but for me the acting lesson was so emotional that I couldn't handle it. I made a vow to go back, because now I am taking an acting and directing for camera class at Laney. I still stuggle with the emotional side, but I will conquer it!

Warriors vs. Mavericks 4/27/07, weare at half time. Warriors are up 13 points. GS 61 Dal 48, 8 turnovers from Dallas. 3rd quarter GS 89 Dal 71. GS 95 Dal 73, 4th 9:03 to go GS 100 Dal 78 4th, 6:15 to go. GS 102 Dal 85, 4th 4:41 to go. GS 104 Dal 85, 4th 4:02 to go. GS 109 Dal 87, 4th 1:53, under the two minute mark. The announcer states that the key turn around for the Mavericks is to defend Baron Davis. GS 109 Dal 91 final 0.0 Warriors now lead it 2 games to 1. They are leading a best of seven series.

Warriors vs. Mavericks 4/29/07, We are at Ricky's. There are 24 people in the main room. There are 14 people at the bar. Erin is bartending with Roxy. They're showing stats on Jason Richardson and clips of the Mavericks. Warriors all-access is next. Shanelle and Derrick and Vern are here for the game. Mavericks have lost 6 of their 7play off games. There is one Maverick fan. First foul of the game, Dallas Mavericks. Tied at 6, 9:18 to go in the 1st quarter. 2 fouls called against Barron Davis. He's the glue to this team, the announcer says. 3rd turn over of the first quarter. The score is Dallas 12 Oakland 6, 6:10 to go in the first quarter. 17 to 10, 7 point lead for Dallas. First quarter 3:34 to go Dallas 17 GS 11. 2:41 to go, 1st quarter 21 Dallas GS 13. End of the 1st quarter Dallas 27 GS 21. It's a six point lead by Dallas, that ain't nothing. The one Maverick fan, his name is Jay. He's still rooting for he Mavericks. Warriors 7/17, 2nd quarter started. Dallas 29 GS 21, 11:06 to go, turn around Barron Davis. Time out Dallas, Dallas 32 GS 27. Dallas 34 GS 29, 7:49 to go. Dallas now 37 GS 33 with 6:08 to go. Time out with 6 minutes remaining in the second quarter. Warriors were the champions in 74-75, Warriors history. Barron Davis is going to the free throw line. 37 Dallas 34 GS. Dallas 40 GS 34. Dallas 40 GS 34, 8 point lead 3:43 to go. 42 Dallas 37 GS. 42 Dallas 39 GS, 3 points. 42 Dallas 39 GS with 2 and a half minutes to play in the first half. 42 Dallas 42 Warriors. 44 Dallas 42 Warriors at the free throw line. 44 Dallas 43 GS. 46 Dallas 43 GS. Dallas 48 GS 46, 0:1 to go. Halftime tied 49 to 49. Pam Oliver is reporting, Dallas 49 GS 49, 11:34 to go in the 3rd quarter. Dallas 49 GS 42, 11:00 to go 3rd quarter. Dallas 49 GS 52, 11:00 to go. Dallas 44 GS 55, 10:31 to go. Dallas 54 GS 55, 9:14 to go. GS 57 Dallas 54, 8:30 to go. GS 58 Dallas 54, 8:13 to go. Dallas 59 GS 58 with 7:12 to go. GS 60 Dallas 59, 6:38 to go. Dallas 60 GS 60, 6:24 to go. Dallas 61 Warriors 60, 5:24 to go. GS 62 Dallas 61, 4:56 to go. Dallas 64 GS 62, 4:30 to go. Dal 66 GS 62, 4:40 tog o. Dallas 70 GS 62 time out with 3:36 to go. Baron Davis gives 25 tickets to the community to come to the game, takes pictures and signs autographed pictures. Dal 70 GS 62, 3:25 to go. Baron Davis has no open shots, and the Mavericks are up by 7. Dal 72 GS 63, 2:54 to go, 9 point lead. 72 GS 65, 2:31 to go. Dal 72

GS 67, 2:04 to go. Dal 72 GS 67, 1:46 to go. Dal 72 GS 69, 1:27 to go. Dal 73 GS 69 with 1:27 to go. Dal 74 GS 72, 1:01 to go. Dal 76 GS 72, 41.1 to go. Dal 77 GS 72, 33.1 to go. Dal 77 GS 75 and the clock is counting down. Dal 77 GS 75, 5.1 in the 3rd and it's Dallas' ball. Dallas 77 GS 77, tied at the end of the 3rd. Shannell helped me with my notes. Dal 77 GS 77 top of the 4th, 11:34 to go. Dal 77 GS 79, 11:03 to go. Dal 79 GS 79, 10:37 to go. Dal 79 GS 79, 10:32 to go. Dal 81 GS 79, 10:17 to go. Dal 82 GS 79, 10:01 to go. Baron Davis is fowled by Jason Terry. Foul against Job, his personal foul. Dal 83 GS 79, 8:50 to go. Dal 83 GS 81, 8:18 to go. Dal 86 GS 81. Dal 88 GS 81, 6:22 to go. Dallas 88 GS 83, 6:01 to go. Dallas 88 GS 86, 5:07 to go. Carlos Santana, Jessica Alba, Ron Artez, and Dusty Baker are all at the game. Dallas 88 GS 86, 4:19 to go. Dal 88 GS 86, 4:19 still to go,4th quarter. Dal 90 GS 86, 3:36 to go. Dal 90 GS 89, 2:53 to go. Dal 90 GS 91, 2:33 to go. Dal 90 GS 91, 2:06 to go. Dal 90 GS 93, 1:155 to go. Dal 90 GS 93, 1:37 to go. Jason Richardson at the foul line, missed. Dal 90 GS 94, 1:02 to go. Dal 93 GS 99, 23.9 to go. Dalllas 93 GS 99, 23.9 to go. Dal 93 GS 99, 16.8 to go. Dal 96 GS 99, 09.9 to go. Dal 96 GS100, 09.9 to go. Dal 99 GS 101, 03.2 to go. Baron Davis 102 to go, Dal 99 GS 103, final score. The next game is Tuesday 7:30 p.m.

Warriors in Dallas 5/01/07 I walked into Ricky's and the Oakland A's won 5 to 4 against Boston. Ricky's is literally standing room only. GS 48 DAl 41, 2nd quarter 10:47 to go. GS 30 Dal 44, 2nd quarter 8:09 to go. GS 32 Dal 44, 2nd quarter, 7:52 to go. GS 32 Dal 53, 2nd quarter 4:42 to go. GS 40 Dal 57, 2nd quarter 3:44 to go. GS 45 Dal 59, 2nd quarter 2:27 to go. GS 50 Dal 59 2nd quarter 52 seconds and counting down. GS 55 Dal 62 Halftime. GS 56 Dal 62, 3rd quarter 10:36 to go. GS 60 Dal 63, 3rd quarter down by 3, 9:39 to go. GS 63 Dal 65, 3rd quarter 9:07 to go. GS 64 Dal 65 3rd quarter, 9:07 to go. Dal 67 GS 64, Dallas up by 3, 3rd quarter 6:02 to go. GS 67 Dal 67 3rd quarter 7:40 to go. Dal 71 GS 69, 3rd quarter 6:40 to go.

7-6-07 I'm siting here with Manuels family and friends. He is the brother of RaiderMan. There all here for his wake. It looked like over a hundred people. They are all so friendly. I've been sitting here for the last three hours working on my How To Kill A Player script. It is so hard now to keep it going. each time I come here to Ricky's I'm able to do 5 more pages. For me 5 is a lot. I told one of his sisters that it is great for them to celebrate together. They said his name out loud and said salute twice. That was so cool. One person yelled out my favorite sound Ay, Ay, Ay, Ay. Now there just talking about the times that they've had and their families. Well I'm just thankful that I can be here, and around other great people.

Just thinking about the Black Hole. Black Hole Rob is the President of that set. I had mentioned to him that if he had someone to back him, he could make the black hole his. They got it together and he's owned the name for a while. The Black Hole is the main group that people ask me about. I know a lot of people. Black hole Steph has been the girl that's my pal. She, Stoner Dude, and Raider Rob were the radio hosts. Mike, Vandamit, Dynomutt, and Mordrid ran the computer chats. They also made sure that the broadcasting was going as planned. They had a lot of guests to give their views about the games as the season went on. Chris Dobbins came in to give his views about the A's. I'm grateful to them for promoting my first book, How to Kill A Player. They let me talk about it and then asked questions. I answered them, head on. I used to go to every broadcast. Then I got to where I was to busy. I worked at least for three jobs and singing karaoke just for fun.

The 66th mob is the tailgate that I would visit before and sometimes after karaoke. Griz is the president of that set. He told a story of the tradition, of the bon fire. It was lit every time they started the tailgate. There is a story behind it, Griz can tell it. Griz would also have different sponsors that he would present in commercials, or just have them to be there for the tailgate. He also had people to contribute to the food for the tailgate, but he has had a lot of people at the tailgate for years. He has always been nice to me. ESPN would always stop by each beginning of the year to film a commercial.

Ricky's is always the place that Raider Fans go to for the beginning of the season. They usually have Raiders Draft day, which is sponsored by the Oakland raiders Booster Club. The draft day always had former players. They had recent players also. I was able to have all the players sign my jersey. Ricky also offered a steak or chicken dinner. They both tasted great. My boys were able to go with me for the 2006 draft day. I was able to make a movie out of that one. I need to upload it to my myspace, Raidercat1.

The main band that plays at tailgate, Rick's, and the A's games is Raiderhed. The band members are Stoner Dude, Dynomutt, Vandamit, and Higher1 Raiderhead usually plays at Ricky's before a home game at Ricky's. I was happy when they gave Raidercat a shout out! They usually have a tip bucket in front of the stage. They are very good! I have listened to a lot of bands in my time and they are at the top of the list. I went to an a's game tailgate and they were there playing. I was invited by Keith. He is a part of the Green Stampede. There are some of my friends that go to the a's games and they are the ones waving the flags. They are very disappointed that the a's will be moving to Fremont. Swisher is my favorite player and a man after my own heart. I have been growing my hair for soon to be eight years now, and I want to go on the Maury show and cut it for kids with cancer.

Chris met with Black Hole Rob and wanted to do something like the Black Hole for the A's. Chris was also teaching and felt that he also wanted to do something for the kids. He used to always take the kids to the A's Games. He felt bad because they couldn't get their school work done. September 10th, 2001 was the first time the students did their homework at the games, and then stayed for the games. In 2002 he got the 501C3 non-profit status. Chris Dobbins is the president of the Green Stampede.

Wayne started the Oakland Raiders Boosters Club in 1996 when they returned. It was originally started in 1961 as the Downtown Oakland Raiders Booster Club. Wayne Deboe is President, Vice President is Peter Berzins, Zina Grant is membership coordinator, Brad Walters is program coordinator, Denise Boxill is public relations, Darryl Dolin is communications manager, Catherine Worth is the recording secretary, Tom Pacheco is in marketing, Charlotte Gonzalez is the project secretary, Dick Ryan is the treasurer, Tom Lyndon is the honorary member, Jenny Hamilton is in special projects, Sean Hamilton is in special projects, and Harvey Robinson is in marketing. The meet ings were held at the west side conference in the Coliseum. The Boosters Club has a yearly away game is planned. The interesting part is meeting people from across the country and then we look for them every year.

I have just be told that Chauncey Bailey has been shot. It was a masked gunman in black clothing. He was shot once in the head. Then the gun man leaned over him and shot him in the head. I just saw him at the Valentine's karaoke show at the Berkeley Reperatory theater, and he told me to watch out because no one leaves channel 2. I can see him now in hios dreds. He asked me to email him the answers to his questions for How To Kill A Player. He used all the information that I typed up. He then added a little bit of his own, and Put his name on it. He went from Soul Beat to being the head of the Oakland Post. I asked him plenty of times could I work for him, writing. He will be missed!

One of the greatest guys to grace Ricky's is George Gray sorry to say he passed February 23, 2007. His birthday was February 24th. He always talked to me before karaoke. He used to talk to ken about the Raiders games all the time. Tina tells me that he was a raider fan who hated the yankees.

There are a lot of children that are brought to tail gate. They are brought to the games. They usually meet all the costume people. I know for me ever since 2002, I have dressed for the children. You know how their faces light up when they see a person in costume. Yes, some may get scared because of the silver and black make-up, but there are a lot who don't. I give trading cards to adults and children. I had one little girl to have me her tennis shoe to sign. That made my world. I like to think that the little girls can look up to a female Raider costume person. I am able to do a lot more greeting than the Raiderets. I love them to death. At one of the draft parties at Ricky's I was able to take a picture with two of them, that were on a button. I was happy that Darryl of the boosters club brought out one of the players to take a picture with me after that. Then my son saw him at the boys and girls club and he remembered me and my son.

Ricky's Sports Grill and Steakhouse is located at 15028 Hesperian Blvd. (510) 352-0200. The email address is www.rickys.com. Tina and Ricky are the owners. There are great waitresses that work here. He also has a great number of cooks that prepare food very well. I have been here ever since 2002. I am sitting here now and the New York Yankees are playing against the Mariners for the wild card position. it's round three of a three game set. There is a tv that has CSTV on and their website is cstv.com. FSN and Bigten are on also. On FSN I guess their having aircraft races. It's the first time I've ever seen it. The aircrafts fly in between this course at speeds up to 85 miles per second, maybe, because the course time is over in 1:32. It's the altometer that reaches to 80+, and they circle the course twice. Mike Golberg and Allen Preston are the commentators. Every Thursday before a home game there is a boosters club meeting. Raiderhed plays at the rallys that they have at Ricky's before every home game. There is an advertisement for The greatest Elvis collection, five hours of Elvis, www.tvatlas.com.

Fred is here at Ricky's and he's been a Raider fan since 1962 or 1963, when the Raiders first came into Oakland. For his birthday his father bought him Raider tickets. He's been a Raider fan ever since. He normally wears his Raider fan and his Raider shirt. Today he has on a different shirt because he spilled mustard on his Raider shirt. He feels different because he doesn't have his Raider stuff on. His friends always say that he has his Raider stuff on. He wears a Raiders shirt vor everyday. He met Jim Plunkett because his mother and father are blind. Plunkett played maybe in the mid 70's? Fred has met all the players on Ricky's wall. He says that Phil Vellapiano and he signed a bottle of wine for him. He met Lester Hayes, and used pine tar to help him grip the ball better. He says that Bo Jackson ran two hundred yards for one game, and it was really incredible. In that same year he hit a grand slam in the all star game. All the players use to come down and sign everything the fans had.

Troy is another die hard Raider fan. He's been a fan since they came back from L.A. They got rid of Randy Moss, and they picked up a hand full of young talent so we'll see what it does. He's doesn't know a lot about the new coach so he wants to see what happens. He is a Raiders' fan because he grew up with them and their the home team. He hopes they take on the talent that they have and utilize it.

John Vella is here with Jim Adams at Ricky's. He was drafted in the second round out of USC. He was an all american in high school and college. His rookie year, first playoff game was the immaculate reception. 2nd year he became a starter in the fourth game replacing Legendary Hall of Famer Bob Brown. He was at the end of his career, and I requested. He had a lot of respect for Bob Brown and when Head coach John Madden told him he would be the starter, the first thing John Vella asked was did John Madden tell Bob Brown. When practice started I didn't want us both being in a huddle at the same time. The highlight was playing in superbowl 11 versus the Minnesota Vikings, when we won the superbowl. I opened Castro Valley store in 1987. I was asked many times why was I opening a Raiders store and they were in L.A. I said that the fans are still here. 20 years later I am still in business, it started as a hobby, and now it's a great business. Jim was friends with Phil Villapiano and that's how we met. They've been long time friends ever since. Jim Adams(National Public Relations Director) has four season tickets next to John Vella, and they have 8 seats together and Jim is from Jersey. They both go on Road games, especially to Miami this year. John Vellas number is 1-866-JVELLAS, for Raider merchandise and Raider trips. If you mention Raider Cat, you can get a ten percent discount.

Mike Johnson is here at Ricky's also. My first experience with the Raiders was at the immaculate reception, December 22,1972 It was pittsburgh and the Raiders, and when Franco Harris caught that ball, tears came down my eyes. 1976 season, Superbowl season, the Raiders won their first superbowl. I remember Willie Brown going down the sidelines with that interception. 1980 playoff game, houston and Oakland, I sat in the third deck. "I was sick and had the flu, but I had to be there." Superbowl against Philladelphia, Kenny King caught the pass from Jim Plunkett. "I was at the house, and the house went crazy!" "The roof was jumping off, Go Kenny! Go Kenny! Go Kenny!" When they were in L.A. and they won Superbowl 18 against the red skins, that was money in the bank. "We whooped they ass." This year 2007, I want them to be competitive, and believe that they can win every game!

At 7p.m. we had our Oakland raiders Booster Club meeting. I was able to get my mediums shirt, club pin, and my raffle tickets. I bought ten dollars worth. I had my video camera ready. The player that came to talk to us was, Tom Howard. He was straight and to the point, and ready for the season. I am very glad to see players, after they have come to the Booster meetings, and then see them in the game. I missed NNamdi Asamougha at the end of last year. He received favorite player. This year I paid for my friend Lover to go to his award dinner. She took a friend from work, and they had a ball. The pictures are on my Raidercat1 page@myspace. They asked was she someone that was important, I told her I hoped she said yes, and that she was there for me. I had to work for Channel two, and couldn't go. She took great pictures with the camera I gave her. I was happy. She has a picture with Nnamdi which is what I wanted. Then afterwards, they came to karaoke at Ricky's and I got my camera, and the story. I had a good time singing.

Yesterday was pretty cool! I went to the Coiliseum, and met Ken to get ready to go to tailgate. We were able to go into the gate at eight o'clock. Then we went into the gate and Pam, Ken, Reggie, and Mike all had the spots taken, so we could set up tailgate. The first thing they set up is the tents. Then they set up the grills. The next thing is to set up all the vegetables. The ticket administration came along with the nfl and game day photographers. Eventually I put my make-up on and went to the Myspace tailgate. I wanted to see them since I have my own myspace. Come and talk to me at www.myspace.com/raidercat1. I have to add some more blogs, which will be soon.

Then we came to the tailgate for Pam, and the rest, to get as many greetings before going in. Then we walked to D gate. The seats were right there. I sit in row 122, row7, seat 1. Right in the front, Oh my gosh, I couldn't believe it. I first heard the booing because the lions came onto the field. Then the Raiders came onto the field. It felt good to see them out there again. It definetely felt weird to be on the other side now.

I met Sapp when I was going home. He backed up, and I told him, I'm not gonna hurt you. I'm just sayin' hi, I'm going home. Then I saw Gallory, I reached out, and shook his hand. I told him that he was taller than he looked on TV, but he had a nice suit on. Ok, back to the game. I was able to see the Raiderettes, that's the time when I was happiest. My friend Etta said, "you love to dance, huh." I was doing the soldierman at the Myspace tailgate, and I was dancing with the Raiderettes, since they were dancing to a lot of hip-hop.

I was able to say hi to Gary, and one of the woman I knew from security. I was able to say hi to another one of my friends at double C gate. I went to the front of the gate and asked an ex boss of mine could she pat me down.

She teased me and asked how come I wasn't working. I told her that I quit and now I had season tickets. Oh yeah, we saw Vella walking around a few times with Jim. Everybody was having a wonderful time before the game. I also wanted to mention Reggie saying the autumn wind. They let the Rookies know that a game is not started without saying the poem at the beginning of tailgate.

Back to the game, I was told by one guy to sit down kitty cat. I told him, "I heard that." Then as the game progressed, he said, "She could have stood up." I couldn't take score because I wanted to see the game. I tried to keep track by just watching, But all I can tell you is that the lions made the first and seconds field goals. Then the Raiders made one, and then another one, and they were ahead by one point. Then the Lions came up and won the game. The crowd kept hollering for the coach to put in Dante Culpepper. I was a little disappointed, but I still have hope that they will show everyone this year that they can win at the superbowl.

Everyone started leaving at about third quarter, and then a lot left, at about the beginning of fourth quarter. I know the rest of us stayed until the end. Then we went back to tailgate. Some people got a chance to eat. I didn't eat anything but a link, all day. I had some cranberry juice, and some diet tea. It wasn't that bad. Then we went to help breaking down the tailgate. It was a long time sort of. We wen't to Ricky's after that, and I was treated to a cheesburger that was humungous. It was funny though because I had asked for Cherry Coke, and the drink tasted like diet all over again. It was great to see Ricky and Tina again. Tina looked so tired. Angie, and two more waitresses were hard at work. They were dealing with the three rooms that were full. On saturday I believe there's a game, and then on Sundays Ricky's has breakfeast. The breakfast is good, it's a buffet.

After work to day with the kids, I am going to go home, and get my battery. I will need it to interview or whatever else. I actually got lucky with a typing class this morning. It's actually giving me time to type. I've wanted to write that book for a long time now, It's called, "What I want to be when I grow up." It's going to be about all of the situation that I have been in being a teacher. Mostly it would be for young people who needed a guide to working around, what it is they want to do with their lives. Then I figured out that it could probably help the adults too.

We are sitting for lunch here at the school. Guess what the conversation is. The MTV awards. It is hillarious, we all agree that Brit just should have had more on. The rest of it is hillarious too. I will be able to watch the repeats by Sunday! It was silent for me, the volume wasn't up. Then I got home, and for got to turn it on. I am waiting for the day to be around as much as I can, as far as Hollywood goes.

Doc Rock is here at Ricky's now. He feels that the offense is doing well. He became a fan in 1971. A mix of the running, short passing game, mixed with the long vertical attempts up the field are just the right mix for success. This year we'll be much happier than last, our defense is solid.

Rick is here at Ricky's. He was a 49er fan and lived in Redwood City. Then he and his wife, Myrla came to Castro Valley in 1999. In 2001 he decided that since he lived in the east bay, he should root for the home team. He always watches the game at home on the big screen. Once in a while they invite friends over, but most of the time they enjoy the game together.

I'm sitting here at the Broken Rack. At 6005 Shellmound St., #160 Emeryville, CA 94608 510-652-9808, www.thebrokenrack.com. Wayne is the owner and Dennise is the bartender, Fabi, and John. I usually come here after work now. especially if I'm going to work at Eli's. They are so very nice. From the owner to the manager, on down. They have great food, great pool, and a smoking area too.

Mica from California State University Eastbay(Formely Hayward) is a third generation raider fan. her office is full of raider stuff. her grandparents took her to the game when they were at Burrell field. They recieved tickets at the fity yard line later on at the Coliseum. She, Her brother, grandmother, and father had to draw which name(person) that was able to go with her grandfather. They had to put the tickets in her grandfather's hat, and they would pick which game to go to.(that's so cute.)

Todd is here at the Broken Rack. He's been a fan since 1970, when he was born. When his mom was pregnant he was in her belly going to the game. The AMC championship game he loved because we won and went to the superbowl. He says that this year has to be better than last year.

Juan is here at the Broken Rack and he says that he's been a raiders fan since fourth or fifth grade. His businees is called Diverse Music International. He's had the business for 10+ years. The last game with the Browns and they called a time out. This year and last year are equally frustrating but they have to win. They always have a great team but they can't seem to make it gel.

Desmond is here at the Broken Rack and he's been a raider fan ever since they came back to Oakland. He always starts every year eager for them to win. His truck is an explorer and he has everything raiders on it. He says that he is a home team person. He will remain a die hard Raider Fan!

When we had karaoke last year at Ricky's, it was fun during football season. We would always come for 8p.m. Then Ken would set up the karaoke. He is the KJ, and is very, very good at his job. He has a good selection of music. Ricky and Tina are the ones who would head the restaurant for the night. The chefs make really make great food. The waitresses were Alli, Roxy, Angie, and.

We all got ready, sat, and waited for Ken to give his speech. He always says that we are supposed to clap when someone comes up to the stage and when they leave. He says that we are not the apollo, or the gong show, and basically we're there to have fun. When I was there I always started the show. It's mainly because I was there when the karaoke first started.

Then we would sing for the rest of the night until 1a.m. We always had fun during the night. The women encourage the men to sing. Yes, ladies there are some guys that are handsome and can sing to. The ones that can really sing to me are the ones who have the courage to go up there and sing. to me it doesn't matter if you can sing or not. it's all if you can have a good time. the best thing is when people act mature enough for the club.

Let me speak on club etiquette! You know that when you go out at night, you should use the manners that your mom taught you. Some people go out and they think that acting rowdy is the thing to do. If you act that way, not to sound like a punk, you close the place down. You may go to jail, and you may get banned from the club. You guys know that you can get away with certain things, but eventually you will get caught! Most of the time they may be waiting to pile up what's going on with you.

Oh yeah, and let me mention Shooters. Denise was the bartender that I would go in and give a hug too. They told me that she had passed away this year. I went and tried to sing I will always love you, and balled my eyes out. I couldn't hang. One guy said for me to sing the song, and I told him that the next time I'd do better. I also told him that he would be happy. Then when he got through, he said, "that's alright."

Shooters is owned by Dave and. They are the nicest people I have met. There is a waitress now, I told her she was Debbie's name sake, her name is Debbie also. During football season, we would sing at Ricky's and then head to Shooters. There was one KJ named Mari, and she would always have me to sing Sarah Smile. I don't know how many people got sick of me singing it. I still love the song, and there were a lot of people who would tell me that I did a great job. I always appreciate all the compliments that everyone has ever given me.

The last game against the Browns was great to see. I was in row 122, seat 1, and had a ball. I sat down most of the game. Afrodesiac,—, and insane raider were standing in the front of the section. I was really tired though. I tried to watch so much of it on the jumble tron. Normally I like to stand up and dance hwen the raiderettes are dancing. Of course I love the music. Jenny

Hamilton is the women of the hour, she plays the music. Thanks Jenny for the help with the season tickets and especially the music!

Emmit "Rocky" Rochelle is here at Ricky's, he is the X-ray technologist/ medical Assistant for the Raiders. He's been working for them ever since 1974. John Madden was the head coach, and it was the superbowl, in Pasadena. That's the one that jogs hie memory. He thinks we'll probably win half our games this year. Out of all the cities tha he's traveled over the years, there's no fans or tailgate like the fans of the Riaders. He been to all the cities of the world.

Dale Die Hard Raider Robertson is here in Ricky's. He's been a fan since 1961, when he was born, and is a life long supporter. He is impressed with Dante Culpepper because of his speed and athleticism. He feels they will do very well this year, and that their a play off team. Please come out and support the Raiders.

Kenneth(my youngest son) has been a Raider fan since birth! He is happy that we are currently ahead in the AFC stature. My favorite fit would be a jersey, his leather Raider jacket, and his Raider hat. He likes the knowledge that he can get from one Raider fan, and he says he learns something everytime.

Jay D is a die hard 49er fan. Patrick Willis and Frank Gore are the players that impress him on the team right now. The 49ers are doing horrible with the offense and the defense is pretty good. Hopefully they can get healthy, win some games, and make a run at the playoff. Don't be fairweather fans, because the 49ers have a history of winning, and when they don't people tend to fall off the wagon.

AfroDeesiac has been a fan for seven years. Thomas Howard is the player that he is impressed with because he's making an impact all across the league. He thinks the team is making a lot of progress and that they are definitely on the right track. Raiderfans are special and thiers no one like us in the whole world.

Ken Webb has been a fan for thirty years. Kirk Morrison is the person that he is impressed by because he grew up in Oakland, and was able to play for his home town team. The offense is very much more effective this year. You need to stick with your teams through good times and bad, because when the good times come, you are able to appreciate it more.

In 2006 I was asked to work on a documentary. I was able to tell the director that I could also be one of the women that she was looking for. The documentary was called, Empowerment or Exploitation: Life of a Sex Worker. Here is my story! This was in my past, and it made me a stronger person!

Traci Gaines Interview—tape 1

[Beginning of recorded material.]

00:00:00. Interviewer: Give me your name, Traci, and spell it for me, first and last.

Traci Gaines: My name is Traci Gaines, T-r-a-c-i Ga-i-n-e-s.

Interviewer: Okay. And now you're a student at Laney?

Traci Gaines: I'm a student at Laney College. I've been there for one year now, and I'm there for media communications, um, TV production.

Interviewer: Were you born in Oakland? Are you a native of California?

00:00:31. Traci Gaines: I was born in San Francisco, and it makes me laugh in a way because I'm a Raider fan. I'm known as Raider Cat. I'm a costume person. And I've most of my life in Oakland, and I think if some people knew that they'd say, ["Ah!"]

Interviewer: Why?

Traci Gaines: Because we always call the 49er fans whiners, and since I was born in San Francisco I usually don't mention that part.

Interviewer: A little friendly rivalry going on. Well, describe to me sort of what stage were you at in your life when you actually decided to consider dancing.

00:01:11. Traci Gaines: When I thought about stripping I was actually on welfare at the time, and, uh, my two boys were about five and six. They're fifteen months apart. And the money just wasn't enough. And I thought that it would be okay to dance, but it didn't work out too well.

Interviewer: Did you have a friend who was dancing? How did you get introduced or what clubs did you decide to dance at or submit an application for?

00:01:42. Traci Gaines: There was a guy at the time who had, uh, introduced himself to me when I was out dancing one night, and he told me to come and see the [guy dance]. We had gotten involved, um, and I went to go see him dance every like two weeks or so for a while. And finally I decided, okay, maybe I can ask him, because I didn't know how to start. He introduced me to a girl I, um—and then I called the guy, and he came to the house and it started from there.

00:02:13. Interviewer: So what was your perception when you went to the gentlemen's club and you're watching these other women? What was you ideas about what that job would entail?

Traci Gaines: Well, when I saw them, like with his act—he actually used, uh, whipped cream [laughs]. That embarrassed me a little bit, but he was good. And he would dance and, um, he had this one song that the women loved, and they all had [unintelligible.]

00:02:42. But I thought to myself, [I did], I thought at the time I love to dance. Um, I didn't mind that people saw my body or whatever, and I figured it wouldn't be too bad. So I decided, okay, maybe I would try it for extra money.

Interviewer: Could you tell your mother? Did your family know?

Traci Gaines: I actually told my mom, and I sort of feel bad to this day. But I just came out and told her, "I'm going to dance. I'm going to strip regardless. I don't care what you say," and she put her foot down and she told me to get out.

00:03:14. And so I had to move to my first apartment, um, which was around the corner from the house. Um, sorry to say, I came to find out it wasn't the greatest of apartments. When I first went in there, there was actually a roach on the cabinets, and I sort of just let it go by and moved in anyway. And I didn't have a lot of furniture, and the boys had their bed but it was just—it was amazing.

00:03:42. Interviewer: Describe your first day on the job.

Traci Gaines: What happened was, um, the guy had come to my house and—I'm sorry to say I can't recall his name now. He would be a little upset if I—if he knew that. But he came to the house, and he—I danced for him. And he was like, "Okay. Great. You can come to the club, um, such-and-such a night." I guess it was a Friday. And it turned out I had to dance in Richmond at the club, in Richmond.

00:04:10. And when I went to the club in Richmond, um, he told me that I probably wouldn't get paid for the evening, that I just had to, you know, like show myself to the men and see what they, how they would react or whatever. Well, it was—it was fun but then, um, it was interesting because of course when it comes to dancing, I love it, you know, and I know whoever sees me dance is going to like it. So when I went out there I, um, did my best and, um, performed, you know, took off the clothes.

00:04:44. That was kind of hard though. [Laughs.] Where you just—where you try to take them off—it's not as easy as it looks. But I had danced so well, um, the guy that told me about the job, the one that I was involved with for a minute, um, he came out and tried to protect me, because the guys were coming up towards me. And he was like, "Give her some money. Give her a tip." You know, and they gave me a little bit, which really wasn't much. And the guy that hired me came out from the back, and he ended up paying me because I was, you know, that good.

00:05:18. And it felt good, but then it was really weird as far as the men because there were so many of them in the club and they were just so wild behind what they had seen. And I just, I kind of couldn't believe it after a while. It was like, you know, what's going on; what am I doing? But I kept going.

Interviewer: When you first talked to the manager, uh, about payment, what did he explain to you in terms of your income potential?

00:05:48. Traci Gaines: The other manager, um—we'll call him M.—he told me that we would get paid every other Friday. And right there and then I kind of thought to myself, okay, well, I don't think I like that too much, but I wanted the extra money. Um, what happened was, uh, we would do three songs, and we were basically going out in what I call a swimsuit, where you never really got, um, uh, naked.

00:06:15. And just one night it really tripped me out because he, um, he told me that I wasn't going to get paid. And I knew it was my Friday to get paid, and I was like, okay, he's [saying] something stupid. I said, "You know what? If that's the case I quit." And he said, "You what?" I said, "Yeah. I quit." I said, "I'm gone." I hung up the phone, and I left. But I had done it for about two months. And that was actually at the club in Oakland that I had quit.

00:06:44. Um, and actually now that I think about it, there were actually two rapes.

Interviewer: So—

Traci Gaines: I just remembered when I said that, and it had, had bothered me for a very long time, but I guess I didn't tie the two together. Um, that—when I was in the club in Oakland there was a guy that I knew that was dancing, and we had gone to school together. And I thought he was okay. One night when I was with him at his cousin's house or his house, I'm not sure, he actually—we actually had sex, but he actually, um—

00:07:24. I think that's what they call sodomize me without me knowing it. He just put it in the back, and I sort of hollered and couldn't believe that he had done that, and I pushed it out. I just squeezed until it came out. And I told him, you know, "Get up. I got to go." Couldn't believe it, you know. And it just kind of makes me upset how people say that it's a woman's fault or whatever.

00:07:48. And I kind of [unintelligible] I think it's really both people's—it's the guy and the woman's fault. So—with the other, um, rape incident I had I was actually staying with my, uh, two boys in the apartment that I was in. And this was after I had stopped dancing, um. One of the guys that was at the club in Richmond, he was really nice to me, and I thought he would be okay.

00:08:17. But he called and said that he was having a party and could he have my address. When he came to the apartment, um, he said he wanted to go in the back room and to take the, um, phone cord out of the wall and to close to the room to the kids, the door to the kids' rooms. And when we went in there, um, he basically wanted to lay down and then he asked me could he have sex.

00:08:47. And I was like, "Well, I guess I really don't have no choice." He said he had a gun. And so we, um, ended up having sex. And at the time I had [unintelligible] on the stove, and I was thinking about pouring it on him. And, you know, I thought about the kids and I just basically tried to keep my cool. And I told him, um, because I sort of have like a sixth sense, and it sort of scares me sometimes, but I said, "Did you come in a brown car?"

00:09:20. And he said, "Yeah, I did. What'd you do, look out the window?" And I said, "No. I just pictured it." I said, "You want to know the other thing I pictured?" And he said, "What?" And I told him I saw him laying in a pool of blood, but nobody was found that had did the murder. And he was, uh, like, "Well, are you going to kill me?" And he was like, "No. Why do you keep asking me that?" I said, "Well, I need to know. You know, I have kids to take care of things to do."

00:09:49. And so, um, he said, "Well, le-let's not talk about that right now." And so we laid there for a minute. And then he asked me to have sex again. Well, in the morning I ended up picking up, my, um—his jacket to go and hang it up, and something fell flat to the floor, and it was a heavy sound. And I said, "Well, what is that?" And he said, "That's the gun." And so I just watched him lean over towards the bed, and he picked up the—whatever it was off the floor and put it in his pocket.

00:10:20. And I felt the jacket. It was heavy. And then I put it on the door. And, um, after that he got dressed and—we got dressed, um, for the morning, and he actually asked me to give him some money. And the only thing I had was $300 in the bank. And the bank was across the street. So we went to the bank, and I wanted so bad to tell the guard in the bank that I had been raped and whatever and if somebody could help.

00:10:52. But I couldn't bring myself to do it. So I just took out the money, gave it to him, and we went back to the apartment. And the first thing he asked me was what was I going to do. I said, "You know what?" I said, "I'm going to go on with my life, and I'm going to go to work." So, um, he got in his car, and he left. And I went in the house, and I got dressed, and I don't really remember now if I took the kids to the babysitter or not, but I did go to work that day.

00:11:23. Interviewer: Did you feel like you couldn't go to the police?

Traci Gaines: Well, I had called a friend of mine, and they told me to call the police. And the, the cops—the police came. And he took a report, but I could only remember the guy's first name. I never really knew his last name. And I could only refer to him as a medium-sized black-skinned man, you know, didn't know many features. And he actually just told me he hoped that I would be okay.

00:11:50. And I told him I'd be all right. And the cop left.

Interviewer: Did you ever see this guy again?

Traci Gaines: I never saw him again. I'm glad I didn't, because I don't know what I would have done. I'm not a violent person but—

Interviewer: And this was someone that you had met through the club?

Traci Gaines: Exactly. He was at the club whenever I danced, and, um, I guess I remember one time being at house.

00:12:21. But, basically, if I remember right, all we did was like play cards and, um, that's about it. That's why he seemed like he was okay until, you know—and then I felt bad too because I had told my cousin what he had done, and she said that he probably just wanted me to [have sex] and wanted the money to get drugs or something. And—

00:12:50. Nobody helped me or whatever. So—

Interviewer: That's hard.

Traci Gaines: Yeah. It wasn't the best experience for me. Besides, every other week I only got 50 bucks.

Interviewer: That's really all you made dancing?

Traci Gaines: [Unintelligible-cross-talk] when I did make it, I ended up paying my friend to keep the kids. So I was stripping to pay a babysitter.

Interviewer: What were you promised in terms of money? Did they say there was a huge potential?

00:13:19. Traci Gaines: [Unintelligible-cross-talk] no—well, they try to make it seem like a huge potential because of the dollars that the guys give or whatever. But, truthfully, in a "black cu—club," to me, guys don't spend a lot of money. And they just basically want to like finger you or feel on you or whatever it is. And it's just—to me, it's not worth it.

00:13:45. And, truthfully, with some women, they end up, um, probably sleeping with guys to make extra money or whatever. But I wouldn't bring myself to do that. I always said I wasn't go to bed with someone just because I was dancing. And, plus, it's too dangerous. You don't know what a person will do. I know one guy I talked to, I told him, I said, "Well, you can give me 400, and I'll think about it."

00:14:12. And I just did that to see what he was going to say. Well, and he said that he had 400 in his truck. And now I was like, well, I don't want to find out what the trunk looks like. [Laughs.] I was like, "No. No thank you." [Unintelligible.]

Interviewer: What was your experience of the other women that were working at the club? What were their stories?

Traci Gaines: Um, there was one dancer, um, who actually [picked a character]—I always think about "Player's Club," um—of the girl that was the head girl. And she would have the, um, dancers to dance in different places.

00:14:50. Like there some times when we did, uh, private, uh, shows. I only remember one, maybe two. Um, and they were saying not to like give out your number and stuff, which was, I come to realize as I got older—it was so they could control where the money was going or whatever. But, um, it's just—it's amazing. It's so many different things that they do, um, the different outfits, the different like—

00:15:22. I forgot to mention I had a banana act, and a friend that [taught it to] me. And so I would basically peel the banana, put it on the floor, and I'd put whipped cream on top and then, you know—that's like giving head to a man. Um, and they just—that was like the few times [unintelligible] when I wanted to get a lot of money. So it was kind of like just a show that you put on [as whether] they're impressed by it or not.

00:15:48. That night, um, there was somebody who had to help me pick up the money. [Laughs.] Uh, but I don't even remember, like, how much it was or whatever. And the other thing that I don't, um, like about it is the fact that all men literally think women are whores when they're dancing. They just really think they're sluts or fast. And as—like as soon as they're here, it's just like, okay, I'm going to deal with her in the way that I want to deal with her.

00:16:18. And, to me, I kind of think it was wrong, because she is trying to find a way to provide for herself.

Interviewer: And her kids or school.

Traci Gaines: Yeah, her kids. School. Or whatever it might be. I don't think it's fair.

Interviewer: Well, there's a lot of feminists who, you know, beyond prostitution and pornography, even view as stripping or any type of sex work as one of the things that promotes violence against women or exploitation of women. Do you think that's an accurate assessment or do you think that some people can use it as a constructive choice to reach a goal?

00:16:58. Traci Gaines: Well, I really think it's exploitation, but I might as well be truthful too. Um, there is other sides to it. There are some women, like one woman that I knew, um—she actually did very well. She had money enough to buy better costumes, and she looked more presentable. She would seem like she was more [classy], but I didn't get a chance to talk to her to see, you know, how [great] it really was.

00:17:25. You know, like in the "Player's Club" movie the girl has a car, and she tells the other girl, "You know, you're only going to have enough money to have a Honda Civic." And I don't know if they get like great cars or other things from men, but I know I didn't. So—

Interviewer: Did you see any women in management roles or sort of owning the clubs or was it mostly dominated by men?

00:17:53. Traci Gaines: Yeah. It seemed as if it was mostly dominated by men. Um, the nights that I was there the only women that I saw, truthfully, were the dancers, the strippers. I didn't see any women as far as, you know—like bartending maybe, once in a while, but that was about it.

Interviewer: Tell me again why did you pursue this work.

00:18:23. Traci Gaines: What I thought was, when I first did it, it was like, oh, I can do this. You know, I can dance. I can take off my clothes. I can—I should be good at that. And I thought that it would be okay. The thing that changed me was once I was around the people. And it was kind of odd because I did not like drink a lot. There are some women who drink a lot and start doing drugs and that are doing, um, more things, hard drugs—cocaine, things like that.

00:18:53. But, for me, I just tried myself—to keep myself straight. I tried to just, um, dance. But it was just, it was really hard, because the guys just really want to feel on you. And they talk about you like in front of your face and—it's amazing. It makes you really feel bad. Even though some people try to say, you know, that it lowers your self-esteem and things that, it makes you feel like you're the greatest person in the world when they give you all the attention that they give you.

00:19:29. But once it turns to negative it's like not the same at all.

Interviewer: There's a lot of, I guess, research or theories about how women get into this work and that a lot have a history of sexual abuse or have been sort of indoctrinated at a young age to then think—you had mentioned, "I can do this. It's okay."

Traci Gaines: Mm-hmm.

Interviewer: Was there anything in your background that made you think—

00:19:58. Traci Gaines: Yeah. For me, um, when I was younger I was molested by my father. Um, sometimes I can't even call him that, because I wouldn't even call him that for a while. Um, when I was about 13 he had taken me into my mom's room, and he actually sucked on my right breast and then put his fingers in my vagina. And some people try to tell me now that that wasn't as bad some women, like a friend of men who used to get sexually, um, assaulted every day by her dad.

00:20:32. But, to me, [unintelligible] child, and it still feels the same way. It was somebody that I trusted who betrayed my trust, and I fought with that for a very long time. Um, also after that I felt dirty trying to take a bath. He offered to wash my back, and I told him no. Of course he had seen me naked, and there was a whole bunch of other stuff up until I was about 18.

00:20:57. He tried to come into the room when I was getting dressed. He offered me oral sex when I was 13. I told him, I said, "No. I guess I'll find out when [I'm a married person]—I mean, when I get married that, how that happens or works." And it's just, you know, a therapist told me when I was younger, um, that that definitely, um, starts women to either sleep around a lot or do things that they aren't supposed to do because of being molested or sexually abused.

00:21:30. And I come to find out that that's true. I've talked to plenty of women who have dealt with, um, harsh situations of abuse and other things like me stripping. And come to find out that most of the time they've been molested by a family member or a stranger.

Interviewer: What would you want other young women to know that are maybe—because I think our culture very much—

00:21:55. Traci Gaines: [Unintelligible] in that.

Interviewer: Well, we certainly as women—we're told our value is in our sexual energy or our attractiveness or these things. I mean, our culture and the media seems to say that, and then is there this myth to about you can make a lot of money doing this type of work.

Traci Gaines: Yeah. I know—I've talked to some young people who have said that they wanted to strip, like as a career that they want to have.

00:22:24. And I still say to this day that it's very dangerous. I don't think it's right. They don't know what they're getting into. I think nowadays people are too trusting. I know, myself, I was too trusting. And when you come into contact with people you never know what they're thinking. They may show you one side, and then they show you a different side which could be worse. And you can definitely get hurt or killed [unintelligible] it, and you have to be careful.

00:22:51. Because luckily I didn't get killed when I was raped, so—

Interviewer: What are the things—you know, I think part of it that women— and you had mentioned this. You were on welfare and there's this lure of being able to make more money because you had two boys. You needed to support them. What do you think women need or what can we as society do to help support women in creating an alternative?

00:23:18. Traci Gaines: Uh, for one, uh, what I thought about was that hopefully one day if I made it I could make a program for women who have been molested or abused and help them as far as work and things like that. Because I think after a while they may not be able to function too well. I've had times to where I've been like approached by guys at work and things like that even though they're not supposed to have sexual harassment in the job, and it still feels the same way.

00:23:49. Um, I just—for black people in general, and the reason I say that is because we pay bills or whatever and don't get, um, high wages—most of us, um, are poor and, um, it's hard for us to get jobs and things like that. And I just wish there was something else out there, because truthfully the—it's still hard for me now. I have the two boys. And I don't have enough money, um, regardless of [unintelligible] my job, [unintelligible] school [unintelligible].

00:24:22. Um, guys really will not just help. They want sex in return, and if you don't give it to them or whatever, then, you know, it's—most people will say, "Well, that's prostitution, getting paid to,"—but it's hard. I mean, you have to have some kind of income some way, and then when you do have it you're only getting paid from check to check.

00:24:49. And you're, you're broke in between the times that you get paid. So it's like you still need [milk], you still need food. The kids may need things for school, bus passes, um, clothes, shoes, whatever it is—and even for yourself. And it's just like—it's really hard nowadays, and I just can't explain it enough for the young girls or women in general.

00:25:17. And then on top of that the single parent, um, thing. Most people [say the baby's momma] now, and I don't like that. I go by single mom. Um, all these guys are usually just basically trying to have kids and have women on their hip for life, just for, to me, free sex. So it's not, um, not easy at all.

00:25:47. Interviewer: Yeah. In talking with some of these advocates, what they talk about is women need housing, and they need childcare and education. And unfortunately a lot of our laws look to either we criminalize or we prosecute. For a lot of women that are in those situations, they don't—if they do encounter violence as a sex worker they would never report it because they are afraid they'd prosecute it.

00:26:16. You know, what are the circumstances? And our government, of course, is really—the new attorney general said that's one of his mandates, that this administration was really going to start cracking down on these types of things. But we're also cutting tuition to college and haven't raised the minimum wage, and it's all these things.

Traci Gaines: Well, also, too, [unintelligible] about the woman where she was, uh, I believe a prostitute, and they made a movie on her.

00:26:44. And she was killing men or whatever. Um, I mean, I hate to say it but I believe in what she was doing, what she was doing was wrong. But I know sometimes how men can be. And they can really like torture you or do whatever, and there's really nothing that most people do. And she actually did—the only thing is that she just went too far, but I don't know.

00:27:15. And they try to say that she can't get out of, um, that situation or whatever. But I've gone, I've—I've tried to go all around in different kind of ways and it still sort of tripped me out because I went, and I volunteered for the school district. I went up in every level, from, um, academic mentor, instructional assistant to aide to the handicapped. Um, listening to [BrianTracy] who was a millionaire, and he said education was the key.

00:27:48. Went to Cal State Hayward, [struggled], um, did it by myself. Come to find out at the end of Hayward I have a learning disability, which is reading comprehension. Um, finished my degree in 2004. I started in '98.

Um, took the CBEST test, um, for a substitute position. Got the substitute position, and I took the CBEST test 19 times.

00:30:22. And my book, it says "How to Kill a Player." Um, the reason this—uh, they have knives in their hand is for men to protect themselves because women may actually do something some day. I don't really want it to be violent, but I knew this would catch people's attention when they saw it. I figured this could be Taye Diggs and LL Cool J and Usher.

00:30:47. And basically it's about just different topics, what kind of players there are, do women look for dogs, men pursuing women. There's alcoholism. There's rape. There's [unintelligible] they want money and all kinds of stuff. Women being [hoes], please, because they always say women are hoes, but guys are hoes too. So—

Interviewer: That's where it seems to be the cultural difference. It's okay. Men are validated.

00:31:16. Traci Gaines: Yeah. They're like superheroes because they sleep with women, do whatever, and everything is okay. And women are just like a lower end of the barrel, and let's not talk about the Adam and Eve thing.

Interviewer: [Laughs.] What role do you think government should play in regulating or eliminating sex work, if any?

00:31:45. Traci Gaines: I kind of wish they could, um. I believe in some states, uh—I believe it is okay, if I remember right. I can't remember where.

Interviewer: Nevada has legalized prostitution. It's certain counties it's legal.

Traci Gaines: Oh, okay. Because, to me, um, at least with stripping anyway, um, they have bouncers. They have, uh, security, um. They have bartenders and things like that.

00:32:11. But I think it would be a safer environment than, um, prostitution. As far as prostitution, I kind of wish it could legal. But then I know the dangers sometimes of the men and the things that they do. So I don't know. But, to me, truthfully, it's almost the same because women trying to get money from men, you know, who aren't prostitutes, you know, always have to [fuss] and say, "No. I'm not a ho."

00:32:39. But at least with a ho she gets her money, you know, and it's only an hour. When it's a regular situation and it's a woman, she's with him all day, all night. [Laughs.] And you don't know how much you're going to get. Oh, and then it's not going to take care of you for like a few months. You know, it'd be for like a loaf of bread and some hot dogs.

Interviewer: Did you hear about the initiative in Berkeley?

00:33:11. They were talking about not legalizing prostitution but decriminalizing it. So instead of incarcerating or arresting women who a lot of people say they're victims anyway, but when you punish them or you persecute them through the legal system it actually makes it worse. So they were saying, "We just don't want to spend any resources incarcerating or arresting people that are prostitutes." But the public voted that down.

00:33:40. They did not support decriminalizing it. Do you think there's some sort of—are we—a sort of a split psyche. Here we are with this billion-dollar industry, but then a lot of people do have this sense of it's not morally right or it should be legislated.

Traci Gaines: That's exactly what I was thinking about. The thing is—the reason I was laughing is because it kind of goes back to the—what I say in the book about players.

00:34:11. It's like I know some people get upset because they find out, okay, my husband [is sleeping around] on me or my boyfriend has been out with somebody else, but it's a hooker. You know, it's like they may be doing it and you don't even know. So either way somebody has to get paid. It works both ways. The person needs to get paid whether they're doing drugs and all that kind of stuff. I remember when I was in Hayward, and we were talking about helping the homeless.

00:34:40. To me it's the same thing. The women are goin—are going to do whatever it is they need to do to, to survive. And if that's what they choose to do, they're going to do it. If they get in trouble behind it, um, I don't know.

What would they do? Put them in jail a certain amount of time before they end up keeping them for good or—that's the part that gets me. Because like how can you put somebody down when you don't have a system for them to get a whole bunch of money or something like that.

00:35:08. People tell me now that [unintelligible]—you know, I say I have a bachelor's, and I'm looking for work and trying to get work, but, uh, I asked them—one woman, I said, "Really? Is it better that I have a bachelor's?" And she was like, "Yeah. It's better. I have a master's, and I'm teaching college." And I was like, "Well, I'll find out." But I have to admit—and I always tell people, and I'm just real about that—I'm black. They took away affirmative action.

00:35:37. They don't have to give us anything now. Before maybe they did say, "Oh, okay. This is one we can take in. Maybe it'll be okay." The only thing that makes me upset is we're not all alike. There are the thugs. There are educated blacks. There are ones who are in between, sort of like me. [Laughs.] There are ones who are middle class. There are ones that are rich. There are ones that are poor. You just have to basically make each individual—meet them and see what happens.

00:36:07. You never know.

Interviewer: Just humanity in general.

Traci Gaines: Mm-hmm.

Interviewer: It makes me think of Martin Luther King, you know, being judged by the content of your character not the color of your skin.

Traci Gaines: Exactly. And I like to think of myself as Martin Luther Kingette, because I tell people all the time what I feel, and hopefully they can handle it. And I always tell people too, I'm not prejudiced. My mom didn't raise me to be prejudiced.

00:36:33. I love my color, and I know [what I'm going through]. There's a friend of mine that's with me now and when we went to certain places, like a computer store, and we went to, um, a video store. And she couldn't believe it. I told her, I said, "Stand there." I said, "Wait and we'll see what happens." I said, "I'll bet you they'll talk to you first." And we just did it to experiment, but it was true. He came to her [snaps] just like this and then come to find out later that she had to send the person to me in order for him to—

00:37:06. And I told him, I said, "Well, right now, I have a lot of money. I want to get a new computer." I was thinking of my film school in San Fran at [unintelligible] and TV production at Laney. But I thought about the service and all that kind of stuff. And I said, "Well, I'll think about it." The same thing happened when I was in the car place. I was ready to get a new car, and I told him, I said, "Well, I'll think about it." It happens at even, um, clothing stores too.

00:37:33. I was ready to spend a lot of money, and this one little girl would not approach me whatsoever. So when the other one did and gave me, um, a hello and a good greeting, I spend big money. She got a good commission that day.

Interviewer: Yeah. They talk about that too just in sex work, that there is definitely racism.

Traci Gaines: It's definitely different. That's what I was trying to say earlier even, and I didn't get the chance. A black club, to me, compared to a Caucasian club or one that's mixed or whatever, yeah.

00:38:04. Or at least it looks like—[at one of] the Caucasian clubs, I was told by someone that they had a buffet. [Laughs.] We didn't have that at the black clubs. Oh, we had the bar, but we didn't have food. Woo, yeah! That was amazing.

Interviewer: Do you think there's any stigma attached to having danced or how do people react to that when you tell them you did it?

00:38:36. You told me your experience with your mom.

Traci Gaines: Yeah. They just—they really do feel like you're trashy. They feel like you're like the bottom of the earth. I put—I always put it like this—when it's your friend, they think it's okay. You know, you, you're providing for your kids. You had to do something. Everything is fine. And I have two boys, um, Kevin and Ken, and they're teenagers now. And I told them about what I had done. And I was like, "I hope you're not ashamed."

00:39:02. And they said, "No. We're not ashamed." And I said [unintelligible] moms have to do whatever they can to take care of their kids. And I think they're pretty good [unintelligible]. But, um, most people, they just really look down on it. It's like, "Oh, you did that?" Or most men will be like, "Oh, I can sleep with you now." You know, it's like a silent—what I call a silent okay or whatever. They just—it's not good, not good at all.

00:39:33. Interviewer: So that's obviously something you don't really reveal to someone you'd be dating, because men kind of categorize then or make a judgment right in that moment of who you are as a person.

Traci Gaines: Exactly. It's like I, I do if I've know the person for a while, like, I don't know, six to eight—six months to a year. Then maybe I'll tell them after a while, um, just to add a little something to the relationship.

00:39:59. But most of the time, like when I first meet them or whatever, no. I don't tell them. Like when [it] came to the interview, you know, there were a few people that I told, and they were like, "Oh, great. You know, that's good because [unintelligible]." But then other people, I was like, well, I haven't told them I was stripping so I can't tell them about the story. [Laughs.] But now it's actually—it's—it gives me a, a big relief because I used to tell the kids, and they were like—they made me feel good.

00:40:29. [Unintelligible] you're going to be president. And I told them, I said, "Right now, I actually could be. I'm more than 30, and I haven't got into too much trouble." And then I started laughing because I thought about the dancing, and I thought about Clinton and what happened with him. And I was like, "Okay. Well, right about now, I actually could. It might make my nomination a little better." [Laughs.]

00:40:55. Interviewer: They had the best inauguration party. [Laughs.]

Traci Gaines: And I wouldn't have to strip. [Laughs.]

Interviewer: Is there anything else that you wanted to add that I haven't asked?

Traci Gaines: Um, basically just, uh, that, um, young women and, um, maybe some middle-aged women could—that, um, stripping to me is not the thing to do. Um, I know there's other things that you could do, especially education. Um, go to college. Um, think about what you like to do.

00:41:29. Even with college, there is an undecided degree, like at Hayward. You don't even have to know what you want to do. You can just go and take the general classes, English, math and whatever else you need to take. And then, by the end of that degree, you can decide what you want to be and make it your major. Um, I still want to—I'll be at school at [Film Arts] when I can. Um, and [unintelligible] for TV production.

00:41:57. And I wanted to go to school for radio broadcasting [unintelligible], but I can't go right now because I don't have the money. But we'll see what happens.

Interviewer: Okay. Thank you, Traci.

Traci Gaines: Thank you.

Interviewer: Can you think of any questions for me? I think you covered anything I asked.

Traci Gaines: Mm-hmm. [Laughs.]

Interviewer: You did great.

Male Voice: There were a few times I wanted to go ooh-ooh-ooh. [Laughter.]

Traci Gaines: You thought of it, huh?

00:42:31. Interviewer: Oh, and I just want to get one thing on camera. Are you still rolling?

Male Voice: Yeah.

Interviewer: I'm going to ask you, "Empowerment or exploitation?" I just want you to go, "Exploitation."

Traci Gaines: Yell it or no?

Interviewer: Whatever you want.

Male Voice: Do you want a close-up on that?

Interviewer: Not too, because I need to cut this with other people. We're going to do a montage at the beginning.

Male Voice: Oh, okay.

Interviewer: Are you framed?

Male Voice: Yeah.

Interviewer: Okay. Just empowerment or exploitation?

00:42:58. Traci Gaines: Exploitation!

Male Voice: Okay. Hold up your [unintelligible-cross-talk]. I want to get a close-up of that so we can [unintelligible] later on.

Interviewer: And the book and all that.

Male Voice: Yeah, I did get the book. I want to get another one of the book.

Interviewer: Okay, great.

Male Voice: Turn the card a little bit. There you go.

Interviewer: [Unintelligible.]

Male Voice: Okay. Move it around a little bit because I'm getting a reflection in there. Wow. Now I see nothing. Down. Turn.

00:43:32. Interviewer: Which way? Left or right for her?

Male Voice: This angle here. I need to get that angle. Yeah. There we go.

Interviewer: Now how did you come up with your character? Did it take you a while? Did you—

Traci Gaines: [Unintelligible] a friend. [Unintelligible-cross-talk] um, costume because we were going to a game.

Interviewer: Oh. And they said, "Hey, do you,"—

Male Voice: Like that.

Traci Gaines: And he asked if I could, um, [get on] and put it on it. And I said of course.

00:44:02. And so what happened was when I first started, I, I was just painting my face. And [unintelligible] like, uh, I'm in the book better to rain in hell, on page 225—

Male Voice: Okay.

Traci Gaines:—um, [laughter], uh, it's about Raider fans and stuff like that. And I was actually talking to a woman from Channel 7 about the water situation. They want, they, they want water [unintelligible]. So that's the difference is you just you have to name yourself and keep going every year and [change the costume].

Interviewer: I've been to an A's game, but I've never been a Raiders game. But I've never even been to Candlestick Park.

00:44:38. Traci Gaines: Really?

Interviewer: No. After nine years.

Traci Gaines: I haven't—well, I don't think I've been to Candlestick Park [unintelligible].

Interviewer: But, see, I grew up also in Dallas. So the 49ers and the Cowboys are not—I mean, I'm not a huge sports person anyway, but you know—not like I follow the Cowboys now, but that was certainly the team that I rooted for growing up. I mean, football is huge in Texas.

00:45:04. I mean, that's what you do Friday nights, all through school.

Traci Gaines: The thing for me is I want to, I really want to travel. I haven't had a chance to travel yet. I've always [been inside] of Oakland.

Interviewer: Where do you want to go?

Traci Gaines: I want to go to the usual places. Some people say Paris. It may be a little difficult, but I want to go to Paris. I want to go to Hawaii. I want to go to, um, Italy maybe. Um, other than that I don't know. [Laughs.]

00:45:33. Interviewer: You could—top three to start with.

Traci Gaines: I'd have to see what happens. I mean, I always ask my friends about passports and—

Interviewer: Those are pretty easy to get and they're good for ten years.

Traci Gaines: Yeah. That's what my friend told me. He said it was good for ten years. So I was like, "Well, maybe I'll get one and still dream."

00:46:57. Traci Gaines: Yeah. And I just—I wish it was [unintelligible].

Male Voice: It's all about self-love.

Interviewer: Yeah, totally.

Male Voice: [Unintelligible] and even if you're a millionaire, some of these people—

Interviewer: We need to go, guys. It's 11:20. We're supposed to be packed up and on the road.

Male Voice: [Unintelligible-cross-talk.]

Interviewer: Okay. One over my shoulder. Okay. All right. That's fine. I just—we are like so—can you have a seat? We're going to get one more over the shoulder from me to you. Maybe me asking you a question.

Male Voice: [Unintelligible.]

00:47:29. Interviewer: Yeah. That's fine. That's fine. You're going with us. Right? Yeah, because we're getting b-roll of you now. And I try to pad this a little so—but I want to make sure everybody gets a bite to eat and we have time to set up in the studio.

Traci Gaines: Have a bite to eat where?

Interviewer: Is there no food over at—well, there's stuff around Laney. Right?

Traci Gaines: Um, they have a cafeteria.

Interviewer: But there's got to be a restaurant or something in a couple blocks, a little café. What's the one? Did you bring—

00:48:02. Male Voice: Oh, on Broadway. On Broadway they've got a great vegetarian restaurant there.

Interviewer: And that's close.

Male Voice: Broadway, 8th and Broadway.

Interviewer: Let's talk about it more as we're packing up.

Male Voice: [Unintelligible] six miles [unintelligible].

Traci Gaines: Let's talk about that. Are you treating? [Laughter.]

Interviewer: Yeah. We're going to feed you.

Traci Gaines: [Unintelligible-cross-talk.]

Interviewer: [Unintelligible] well, he eats a lot of raw foods.

00:48:29. Traci Gaines: [Unintelligible-cross-talk.]

Interviewer: I think—well, we're—oh, well, I don't know. We can go someplace that has both.

Traci Gaines: Well, I'm just—I'm just saying, I'm not a vegetarian.

Male Voice: Are you open to trying it?

Traci Gaines: You picked a person that [doesn't like vegetables].

Interviewer: Oh, really. At all?

Male Voice: Do you like gumbo?

Traci Gaines: Yeah.

Male Voice: They make a gumbo down there, you won't even miss nothing. I'm telling you.

Traci Gaines: I'll try it.

Male Voice: Okay.

Traci Gaines: My friend [unintelligible] helped me with that. We used to go out and eat, and she would [unintelligible] that.

00:48:56. Interviewer: Right.

Traci Gaines: I'm one of those people, of course, you know, [we] don't usually try much of anything outside of the culture.

Interviewer: Oh, well, you're going to have a—

Traci Gaines: [Unintelligible-cross-talk.]

Interviewer: Well, good for you. I did that with my niece. We went to this Italian restaurant, and they brought this cheesecake with like the raspberries on it and whatever. And she just—yeah, she had this like scowl on her face. And she was—

Traci Gaines: [Unintelligible.]

Interviewer: Well, it was just looking at it. It was like, "Ooh, no, I don't want,"—and I told her—

00:49:27. I said, "Marguerite, you know, this is part of life. It's not that you have to eat all of it, but just try it. And then you'll know, I like it or I don't like it." She ate almost that whole thing. And I'm like, just open yourself up to—

Traci Gaines: I know. I know. But you should have saw the kids. It was so funny. I told him, I said, "I'm going to expose you to a whole bunch of different music." And they were like, "Oh, Miss Gaines,"—they said, "No. We're not going to listen to KMEL every day." [Unintelligible] turned on classical, and boy, they got [laughs]—

00:49:56. Interviewer: They didn't like it?

Traci Gaines: I'm going to expand your brain.

Interviewer: Yeah?

Traci Gaines: [Unintelligible] listen to it. Plus, people say that it makes you smarter. And they were taking a test, so I ended up playing it while they were—

Interviewer: Taking the test? Yeah?

Traci Gaines:—[unintelligible-cross-talk.] It was [cool]. It was so funny. They were like—and then I played the, um, Spanish channel.

Interviewer: Right.

Traci Gaines: Because I, I can speak Spanish. Um, I took it for eight years.

Interviewer: Oh my God. That's—

Traci Gaines: [Unintelligible-cross-talk.]

Interviewer: But you're conversational?

Traci Gaines: Well, no. I always tell people I speak broken Spanish.

[TAPE ENDS.]

www.ingramcontent.com/pod-product-compliance
Lightning Source LLC
Chambersburg PA
CBHW021257280526
45784CB00005B/2408